THE LIFE CYCLE OF WEALTH

THE LIFE CYCLE OF WEALTH

THE FOUR PHASES OF YOUR FINANCIAL LIFE

AARON KOLKMAN

TATE PUBLISHING
AND ENTERPRISES, LLC

The Life Cycle of Wealth
Copyright © 2014 by Fidere Media, LLC. All rights reserved.

No part of this publication may be reproduced, stored in a retrieval system or transmitted in any way by any means, electronic, mechanical, photocopy, recording or otherwise without the prior permission of the author except as provided by USA copyright law.

The opinions expressed by the author are not necessarily those of Tate Publishing, LLC.

Published by Tate Publishing & Enterprises, LLC
127 E. Trade Center Terrace | Mustang, Oklahoma 73064 USA
1.888.361.9473 | www.tatepublishing.com

Tate Publishing is committed to excellence in the publishing industry. The company reflects the philosophy established by the founders, based on Psalm 68:11,
"The Lord gave the word and great was the company of those who published it."

Book design copyright © 2014 by Tate Publishing, LLC. All rights reserved.
Cover design by Allen Jomoc
Interior design by Jomel Pepito

Published in the United States of America

ISBN: 978-1-62994-532-3
1. Business & Economics / Personal Finance / Money Management
2. Business & Economics / Personal Finance / Retirement Planning
15.04.27

Overview

In the digital era, we receive an overflow of information about how to handle the pieces that complete the puzzle of our financial lives. Eventually, handling the big picture becomes nearly impossible without three key ingredients: (1) clarity, (2) knowledge, and (3) perspective. Clarity means understanding of what is generally most important to you, knowledge refers to the information needed to make great financial decisions, and perspective speaks to the viewpoint from which those decisions are made.

The Life Cycle of Wealth aims to provide both clarity and perspective. However, this book is not a technical manual on personal finance or a how-to guide for the intricate details in a financial plan. Indeed, the complexities of true planning are best managed in a conversation with your trusted advisor(s)—the people who *insert* the technical expertise to improve your outcomes. As you proceed in a planning relationship with financial, tax, and legal professionals, *The Life Cycle of Wealth* will give you an improved ability to make decisions with those advisors.

For those privileged to have already attained their version of the American Dream, this book offers important insights into the challenge of leaving a legacy. For those who have not yet reached the summit of their goals, *The Life Cycle of Wealth* offers a glimpse at the terrain ahead, and a simple approach to navigating your financial landscape with confidence. Above all, *The Life Cycle of Wealth* provides a fresh outlook. Its application allows you to understand the predictability of your financial situation, so you can finally tune out the overflow of information and tune in to your unique calling to greatness.

ABOUT THE AUTHOR

Aaron Kolkman is a retired securities principal and co-developer of *The Life Cycle of Wealth* model. He previously worked for three major US financial institutions before founding a portfolio risk management firm during the 2008 financial crisis, now part of the renowned planning company, Private Wealth Management of St. Louis. He is the creator and host of Strategy Session Radio, a personal finance program aired live on AM1570 KYCR in Minneapolis/St. Paul, and distributed nationally via podcast.

Kolkman is a recognized risk management leader in the area of mean variance optimization (MVO) for retirement income planning with portfolio assets. His Minneapolis strategic planning practice incorporates all phases of the Life Cycle, with a special focus on written estate strategies. Kolkman is a CERTIFIED FINANCIAL PLANNER™ and an ACCREDITED ASSET MANAGEMENT SPECIALIST™. He is a member of the Committee for the Fiduciary Standard, the International

Association of Advisors for Philanthropy, and the Financial Planning Association.

Certified Financial Planner Board of Standards Inc. owns the certification marks CFP®, CERTIFIED FINANCIAL PLANNER™, and CFP® (with flame design) in the US, which it awards to individuals who successfully complete CFP Board's initial and ongoing certification requirements.

The AAMS® or ACCREDITED ASSET MANAGEMENT SPECIALIST™ marks may be used only by persons who have received written authorization from the College for Financial Planning to use them.

DEDICATION

Dedicated with gratitude to my own family tree—the generations past, my parents, my children, and the generations to come.

Acknowledgments

Special thanks to my father, a true giver, whose support has been unending. Your actions continue to speak louder than words to those around you.

Special thanks to my mother, whose loving support and academic expertise have helped bring this project to fruition. Your faith and wisdom speak volumes to others.

Special thanks to the team at Private Wealth Management in St. Louis, Missouri, for their friendship and their insights. This model would not exist without you.

Special thanks to my friend Diane, whose financial support made this book possible. Your belief in something greater than yourself is what this book is all about.

Table of Contents

Foreword 15
Preface 17

A Means to an End
    Money as a Universal Language 21
About the Cycle
    Understanding the Life Cycle Model 27
Phase I: Prepare
    The Infrastructure of Your Financial Life 37
Phase II: Produce
    Using Your Income to Fund Your Assets 43
Phase III: Prosper
    Using Your Assets to Fund Your Income 47
Phase IV: Preserve
    Structuring and Funding Your Legacy 51
Managing Risk
    Recognizing the Pitfalls in Your Plans 59

Finding Your Fiduciary
The Secret to Mastering the Life Cycle 71
Creating Recurrence
The Multigenerational Wealth Challenge 83

Appendix I –
Quantitative Analysis of Investor Behavior
(Dalbar, 2013.) 91
Appendix II –
Questions to Ask a Financial Professional 93
Appendix III –
Financial Designations 95
Bibliography 97

Foreword

If you believe that wealth is a universal concept across cultures, geographic areas, politics, religion, and business, then you can begin to appreciate the incredible influence it has over the decisions we make, the relationships we maintain, and ultimately, the kind of lives we lead. If you cannot accept wealth as a universal concept, this book is not for you. Also, if you steadfastly believe that wealth-building as an end in itself is a worthy pursuit (independent of other objectives) or if you are interested in a short-term method of furthering your financial status, this book is sure to disappoint you.

"There is no shortage of wealth in the world, only a shortage of perspective about it."

—Anonymous

Preface

The pursuit of wealth for its own sake can be destructive. It can de-prioritize faith, relationships, and community. It can create a culture of takers versus a spirit of giving. It can pretend that financial resources alone can fix any problem and deliver one to a better place. On the other hand, pursuing wealth as a secondary consideration is typically noble. If you chart a career path, follow it long-term and fill it with hard work and determination; any wealth you create in the process is probably the fruit of your labor. Stated differently, if you use your gifts, education, and experience to make a contribution to your community, any net financial gain you realize is usually a result of your contribution.

Some critics of this book will say that wealth-building for its own sake is a positive pursuit because it leads to other positive outcomes in life. What are those other outcomes? If having wealth leads to other desired outcomes, then building wealth must be a means to an end. Being wealthy, then, is a secondary objective. When treated as such, building financial resources becomes a *consequence* of you employing your talents, pursuing your dreams, and following your chosen path with discipline.

In his book *Simple Wealth, Inevitable Wealth* (Nick Murray Company, Inc., 1999), financial advisor Nick Murray said, "Wealth is an income you cannot outlive, the absence of financial worry, and a legacy for your children and grandchildren." Mr. Murray's work is based on the long-term financial outcomes derived from Phase II (Chapter 4)—our income-earning years—and proposes a method of growing wealth by systematically investing for growth over a lifetime. Mr. Murray also stresses principles of behavioral finance requisite to investor success with these types of investments.

Appropriately, Mr. Murray's wealth definition revolves around the need to be *financially established*. For the remainder of this text, wealth will simply mean becoming *financially established*. So how does one become financially established? Consider the many excellent publications written about developing wealth in a systematic fashion: *The Millionaire Next Door, Rich Dad, Poor Dad, How to Win Friends and Influence People, Think and Grow Rich,* and *The Greatest Salesman in the World*, to name a few. These books provide tremendous wisdom around building wealth through excellent habits, strong relationships, and sound decision-making. Many of these works have influenced the ideas presented in The Life Cycle of Wealth.

However, The Life Cycle of Wealth is quite different. It is not based on any particular investment approach, personal habit development, or investor behavior management method. Instead, it speaks to the viewpoint we must hold in order to develop good financial habits and execute a risk management strategy. It allows us to engage in superb decision-making—a common characteristic of those who achieve lasting wealth in their lives. So instead of providing a predetermined solution for success, The Life Cycle of Wealth offers us a way of thinking about our financial lives.

With the Life Cycle model, we can see the process of becoming financially established is not only possible, but predictable. This process unfolds in a specific pattern that, when accepted, offers freedom from the directionless existence that can dominate our complex, modern-day regimen. Unlocking that freedom is the primary reason for The Life Cycle of Wealth.

The Life Cycle model is intentionally just a picture—a picture of what it looks like to successfully work through the process of becoming financially established. The picture is flexible and forgiving. It is holistic and complete. It is simple and open. And while its meaning and utility are different for everyone, its value is the same. The Life Cycle of Wealth invokes perspective. With that perspective comes an incredible peace.

A Means to an End

There is only one universal language. It is not spoken. It is not political or cultural. It is certainly not religious. It is economic. Not in the sense of a national GDP, data trends, etc., but in terms of our personal economy or "lot in life." Indeed, the only language known by everyone on earth is *financial*.

The Life Cycle of Wealth deals with this universal language in a relative sense. Consider that "a lot of money" means something different to almost everyone. For instance, those in the lower or middle classes may actually have a very average net worth, but "feel" wealthy. Some top-income earners, meanwhile, may be considered poor by their peers in terms of assets and net worth.

An example: I once did financial planning for a couple in Phase II who had an $80,000/year budget. Their primary goal was to build a $2,000,000 nest egg with which to enter Phase III. This goal included (1) preserving the value of the $2,000,000 through Phase III and Phase IV and (2) funding all of their $80,000 budget without accounting for social security benefits. So for them, being wealthy meant having a 4% income from $2 million and an annual inflation-adjusted total return high enough to render a positive return after fees and expenses on a long-term basis. *Their ability to be financially established hinged upon their ability to meet their budget and preserve their capital for a lifetime.* While this $2MM in assets is a significant sum, there are many affluent families who would not consider it wealth.

Another example: A couple in my practice recently entered Phase III requiring $60,000/year for the first 10 years of this phase, then $45,000/year for the remainder of *both* of their lifetimes. The asset base required for them to be "wealthy" is a present value of around $1.4 million. If this couple had the $1.4 million in assets, they would be considered wealthy in terms of their financial establishment. However, for the previous couple needing $80,000 throughout Phases III and IV, $1.4 MM would be a good start, but certainly not real wealth.

A final example: I once worked with a Phase II client who inherited a sum of $500,000 but needed a $50,000 annual income to live comfortably for the remainder of her life. This inheritance was not sufficient to make her wealthy because the roughly $1.25 million asset base required to fund her Phases III and IV had not yet been achieved.

In each of these examples, the people involved had unique lives and therefore distinctly different definitions of financial establishment. However, their experiences of moving from one phase of their Life Cycle to another was quite similar—and so were the risks they faced. Another common element across these examples was the stress each client carried, not because they faced adversity or had to manage risk in their Life Cycle, but because they were anxious about their financial outcomes.

The Life Cycle of Wealth

This stress comes out in a number of different ways. Common symptoms include: "Where should I put my money?" or "How can I get a better return?" or "I pay too much in taxes." This general financial anxiety illustrates the need for a comprehensive financial strategy.

With a detailed overall strategy for handling their investments, insurance, retirement, estate, and tax considerations, review meetings with each of these clients found them all more confident and less anxious. However, each later admitted to additional worry about their finances. While some ongoing financial pressure can be healthy and productive, this perpetual worry causes anxiety and impacts couples, families, and business partners. It can even lead to poor financial decision-making.

Two of my close colleagues have acknowledged that their clients worry more about financial matters more than they would like. Each of those professionals is well-educated, experienced, and highly regarded in their communities as outstanding practitioners. Yet each of them admitted their clients do not sleep as well as they should. One discussed how a few of his clients have attended a social event and left questioning parts of their own strategic plan enough to believe they should change course in favor of a new approach. Another discussed how some of his clients would listen to a mass-marketed financial show about the latest investment product or holding and often come away convinced they should own it.

Both advisors stated that between review meetings, some of their clients became doubtful and stressed to nearly the same degree as when their advisory relationship had begun, despite having a sound strategy, making informed decisions in meetings, and making marked progress toward their financial objectives.

Indeed, this pervasive recurrence of financial worry is the norm in our culture, certainly during challenging economic times. Its source? According to both advisors, the financial stress their clients experienced simply amounts to a lack of *perspective*.

So how can it be that a universal concept like *money* suffers from such a terrible lack of perspective? The answer lies in how we relate to it. To simplify the analysis, let's consider three distinct financial types, each with a unique way of relating to money and, therefore, a unique method of attaining wealth.

The Givers are the first group. They are the people that think and act for others, often putting themselves out to make a contribution. They seem to do so effortlessly, often with utter disregard for their own needs. They are typically successful spouses and business partners for this very reason. They are also wonderful parents. And when it comes to financial concerns, they are an incredibly generous group, limited only by their own balance sheet and income statement.

The Takers are the second group. This group is easy to spot, and they stand in stark contrast to The Givers. Their self-serving mentality makes sure their own needs are met before they make a contribution. They are usually very comfortable with their disposition and seem indifferent when they put someone else out. The Takers are often excellent business professionals and may climb the corporate ladder faster than their peers. Unfortunately, they can often be less successful in their personal lives as spouses and, perhaps, parents, as these roles require a regular selfless contribution.

The Takers are the group who tend to idolize wealth because it is their nature to do so. They are the people we often regard as "greedy" because they will use their taking nature to pursue a financial agenda at the expense of others. It is common to find

Takers unhappy with their lives. By seeking wealth for its own sake, they develop an insatiable appetite for financial gain and quickly become miserable as their need for affluence becomes more and more central to their existence. They are also miserable because they're attempting to force themselves upon a process that is already a natural inevitability.

The Pretenders are the third group, and the most difficult group to recognize. This is a group of Takers disguised as Givers. They appear as Givers, but cleverly take from others in order to further themselves or their agenda. Although they are truly Takers, the Pretenders have more self-awareness than traditional Takers—enough to recognize they must appear giving in order to succeed in certain areas of their lives. The Pretenders are also often highly successful in business. They may or may not be successful family people. In general, they are a confusing group to interact with because they lead others to believe in their goodness, only to further their own cause.

Being a Giver, a Taker, or a Pretender is not a determinant of success in navigating the *Life Cycle of Wealth*, but it does speak to how predisposed or open we are to using it. The Givers normally demonstrate great ease in navigating the Cycle, while the Takers and Pretenders are often skeptical of the model or even misunderstand the concepts altogether. This is because complete use of Cycle is not a short-term process. It is a journey—a journey based upon your contribution to society in general, with the by-product being financial success. Takers and Pretenders are generally more accustomed to wealth as an end in itself and so have difficulty reaching the financial freedom involved in using the Life Cycle model in their own lives.

So how can you distinguish between these three financial types? Consider the example of a not-for-profit, charitable organization. Many nonprofit charities employ Givers: talented, educated, yet modestly paid workers who spend a career trying to better the community around them in some way. There are donors for these organizations who are equally Givers: philanthropic with their time and financial resources. There are also many Takers and Pretenders who donate time or money to the charity for the good publicity or the tax benefits involved. Unlike the Givers, their contribution was made with the requirement that they or their organization benefit from their own actions, such as good publicity, tax benefits, or networking opportunities.

Whether you identify with the Givers, the Takers, or the Pretenders, there is something to be gained for you from the Life Cycle. With it, you can begin to view money as a universal concept and a means to an end. This viewpoint offers freedom from uncertainty about the future and contentment that comes from knowing what to expect in the years ahead.

So you can begin anew the way you think about your financial life. You can step back and see the predictability of your own path—your current stage and your future steps. You can even see the lifelong nature of the Cycle, with a centuries-old pin oak tree providing a reminder of the larger multigenerational pattern of which we are a part.

About the Cycle

In our high-tech, fast-paced environment, it is easy to get distracted by the short-term chaos happening around us. We can videoconference with business partners in a foreign country, catch the current news on our smartphones, and send a few e-mails on our computers—all in the course of a lunch hour. Indeed, the level of complexity with which today's successful professionals and families live is unprecedented in modern history. As a result, we must have a mental picture of the direction we are traveling. Without it, our daily routines can become a series of meaningless transactional activities that leave us burned out and craving something more.

So what does the Cycle do exactly? It is easier to understand what the Life Cycle does by first understanding what it doesn't do. Here is a short list of the functions the Cycle does not serve:

1. The Life Cycle framework does not offer a short-term method of accumulating wealth.

2. The Life Cycle does not propose one financial strategy over another.
3. The Life Cycle does not refer to any financial product(s) or service(s).
4. The Life Cycle does not provide a behavioral finance methodology.

Instead of these common themes in financial literature and financial services offices, the Life Cycle provides a decision-making framework to navigate your overall financial life. Consider this example: if you try to determine the proper life insurance program for your family or business, there are numerous methods by which to calculate your need for benefits. Once you establish the need for benefits, there are countless health, lifestyle, and financial considerations involved in finding the correct contract—which must be customized based on your own Life Cycle (i.e., your current phase, your timeframe to the next phase(s), etc.). This unfortunate reality exists with any insurance, investment, or other financial product decision you make during your lifetime. In fact, making good product decisions requires you to have a mental picture of your own Life Cycle. It requires you to have a strategy.

Knowing the difference between a *product decision* and a *strategy decision* goes a long way toward proper application of the Cycle to your own financial life. The following paragraphs further illustrate the dynamics of product and strategy decisions. As you consider these points, remember that a financial product is any instrument that meets a specific need. A financial strategy is the overall *direction* of your financial affairs. In short, products are the pieces that make up the strategy puzzle. Great financial decision-making requires that you (1) have a strategy, (2) know whether a given decision is regarding a product or your strategy and (3) if you are making a product decision, whether or not the product fits with your overall strategy. So ask yourself: do I have a strategy? Am I making a product decision or a strategy decision? If this is a product decision, does it fit with my overall strategy?

Making Great Product Decisions

If the product decision involves a trusted advisor who was first engaged for reasons other than proposing products and who is focused on the successful completion of your strategy, reviewing the pros and cons should be a matter of communicating with your advisor. However, if you are making a product decision separate from a strategic advisor, there is often a salesperson involved, and it is essential to review the pros and cons objectively.

The following is a short checklist of questions you can ask when making product decisions for yourself, your family, or your business. Applying these four questions to any product decision you make will greatly improve the clarity with which you proceed.

1. Which of the four phases am I in?
2. Will this product impact my current phase?
3. Will this product provide the desired long-term effects to future phases?
4. In what manner and how much am I paying for this product?
5. What are the risks involved?

Product decisions are generally much easier to make than strategy decisions. While they require you to have a good understanding of the product itself and its risks/rewards, these decisions do not typically require you to evaluate changes to the overall well-being of your family or business in order to proceed. A strategy decision, on the other hand, requires a much longer, more complex decision-making process.

Making Great Strategy Decisions

If you are unsure about what type of decision you are making, remember that strategy decisions do not usually start with a product discussion or a transaction. Examples of questions requiring a strategy decision would be: "At what age can I reasonably afford to retire and not outlive my money?" or "How do I efficiently transfer wealth to future generations?" Think of strategy decisions as "big picture" decisions.

So why have a strategy at all? Why not just find the products and services you need when you need them? Psychologist David Campbell, PhD, titled one of his most popular books, *If You Don't Know Where You Are Going, You'll Probably End Up Somewhere Else* (Thomas More, 1974). In it, he said "When you are planning your future, you should plan it in a way that will give you some choices, and this is particularly important if you aren't really sure right now what you want to do. Some people when they are uncertain have a tendency to do nothing, and this substantially restricts their future choices." Dr. Campbell's observations are hard to dispute, however incomplete. His comments do not address the importance of having plans that are *written*. Consider the following study that demonstrated why written plans are so essential.

In 1979, a group of researchers interviewed new graduates from Harvard's MBA Program and learned the following details:

- 84% had no specific goals at all
- 13% had goals but they were not committed to paper

- 3% had clear, written goals and plans to accomplish them

In 1989, the researchers again interviewed the same graduates. As you might expect, their research found the following:

- The 13% of the class who had goals were earning, on average, twice as much as the 84% who had no goals at all.
- Even more surprising, was the 3% who had clear, written goals were earning, on average, ten times as much as the other 97% put together.

Source: *What They Don't Teach You in the Harvard Business School.* (Mark McCormack, Bantam, 1984).

Dr. Campbell stressed the need to develop a plan and avoid the great risk of doing nothing, while Mr. McCormack emphasized that our plans need to be written. When it comes to having a written financial strategy, though, the process can be daunting. Anyone new to such a process asks questions such as: *What information is needed? What tools should be used? Is it just about the money? What about values?* While there is no right way to handle a strategic planning process, being aware of a few mental pitfalls can help avoid larger problems down the road and allow a complete process to happen.

Planning Pitfall #1: I did it online. There is a common perception among do-it-yourselfers that comprehensive strategic planning is possible using self-directed tools on the Internet. To be sure, there are many planning *modules* you can find online, many of which will give you meaningful information about your financial life, from taxes to investing to insurance, even retirement. However, in my fourteen years of financial industry experience, I have yet to find a single self-directed planning platform for individuals, which is capable of delivering detailed, comprehensive strategic financial plans. The absence of such a tool may be due to a lack of desire or training for end users to navigate it. After all, such a tool would be similar to an architectural firm offering online blueprints for homes based on someone's preferences. Without end users becoming home builders, it is doubtful that many would take the necessary steps to construct the home themselves. Even with proper training and years of experience, would someone want to spend their time and energy this way? Or might it be better to hire someone with the proper training and experience to build the home according to their wishes?

Planning Pitfall #2: My product salesperson does planning. To follow the previous analogy, this would be akin to saying, "My electrician did the blueprints and overall construction of my home." It is true that your electrician may do planning *activities* related to their area of expertise; however, this is also *modular* in nature and does not assure the overall plan is sound.

Planning Pitfall #3: My portfolio is in good shape. This statement implies that investing and strategic planning are one in the same. Investment planning is indeed a form of planning. However, this is also a *modular* form of planning—just like taxes, insurance, retirement, and estate planning. Keep in mind that having a good portfolio or investment plan does not mean the same thing as having a well-written overall strategic plan.

Take the recent example of the late actor James Gandolfini who passed away at age fifty-one with an estate worth approximately $70 million. It is possible that Mr. Gandolfini had a terrific investment plan. However, without a comprehensive strategic plan, the investment-only plan would have done nothing but contribute to an already large estate tax bill of around $30 million in federal tax.

Another word about investing: it is unique from other modes of planning given it can make or break the funding of your overall strategic plan: a successful investment plan can positively impact your overall strategic plan and an unsuccessful investment plan can negatively impact the big picture. As such, it is essential to get outstanding advice in this area. When you do seek investment advice, be sure to remember the difference between trading and investing. Trading refers to using the financial markets to do regular transactions—taking substantial risk in an attempt to generate short-term profits. Investing refers to using financial markets to match your preferences and risk tolerance with a strategy to generate consistent long-term results and, in doing so, fund your entire financial strategy. Comparatively speaking, then, investing is a low-risk method of developing long-term financial establishment.

Planning Pitfall #4: I am already financially established. This is probably the most dangerous mind-set to take regarding financial planning with established resources. It suggests that those resources will not dissipate: be spent in a lawsuit, lost to medical bills, paid out in taxes, squandered, or poorly invested. Especially if established resources are closely held business assets, the idea that of being "set" without a drafted strategy is likely to have negative consequences.

A friend of mine named Darren is a recently retired general contractor of thirty years. Darren had a written strategic plan, but was still disappointed in his income results when he decided to retire in 2009. He simply did not have the assets he expected to have from which to pay himself. His corporation was worth substantially less following the real estate and construction boom, which had peaked in 2006, and his personal financial assets had lost value during the 2008 US financial crisis. To make matters worse, his strategic plans did not account for two important facts: (1) the appraised value of his business meant the company represented over 40% of both his asset allocation and net worth (he had no debt), and (2) the economic conditions at his retirement meant that his business was difficult to sell and even more difficult to sell anywhere near its appraised value.

So planning with business assets means addressing high-risk illiquid assets on the balance sheet. In Darren's case, he did eventually sell his business, although for much less than he hoped. Had he not, his estate would have carried significant liquidity risk. Although such an issue is beyond the scope of this text, it is important for successful business owners to recognize that they have liquidity issues (and perhaps related tax issues) in their estate plan that must be addressed in a detailed fashion. The alternative can be disastrous for beneficiaries.

So strategy decisions need to be based upon a written plan. The plan should be drafted and managed with competent, trusted advisors who make a full-time living providing the right guidance on big-picture issues. When you go to write a check for advice, remember that getting quality advice at critical moments throughout your life will usually bring financial outcomes that far outweigh any fee you paid along the way.

Meanwhile, the following is a short checklist of questions you can ask when making strategy decisions for yourself, your family, or your business. Applying these five questions to any strategy decision you make will greatly improve the clarity with which you proceed.

1. What do I expect to accomplish during this phase?
2. What does the next phase look like?
3. When do I realistically expect to enter the next phase(s)?
4. What are the current financial considerations that come into play?
5. Who are the other people that my decision(s) will impact?

Remember, there is often no "right" answer to a given financial decision—regarding a product or your strategy. Each situation is as unique as the people involved. Herein lies the value of having the clarity and perspective provided by the Life Cycle mindset.

If you commit the Life Cycle to memory, it can direct your thinking. If you use it to approach your own situation, The Life Cycle can provide a decision-making framework, even inform your daily choices. However you use it, including it in your thinking about your financial life will keep you aware of the big picture and allow you to focus on the important aspects of your life without the stress of uncertainty about the future.

Phase I: Prepare

During the first phase of the Life Cycle, there is a financial quiet period. Too often, professional advisors do not engage younger adults, due in part to the perception that younger adults do not have sufficient assets and/or income to warrant any modular or comprehensive strategic planning. This could not be further from the truth. If cash flow (the largest phase risk at this point, see Chapter 7, "Managing Risk") can be well-managed, there is no better time to build infrastructure and cement it with great habits. Here are four critical steps to create the infrastructure needed to complete your strategy in the phases ahead: (1) get organized, (2) develop a routine, (3) insure the future, and (4) install an initial estate plan. Like the other phases of the Life Cycle, there's no right approach to these pieces, only a requirement that they be addressed. The following details provide more insight into each of the four steps.

Step #1: Get organized. Set some initial life goals. Where do you want to live? What are your career objectives? What type of family life do you want to have? This gives context to your financial life. Be sure not to apply numbers to these discussions until *after* you have clarity on what you wish to accomplish.

Create a household budget. Whether it's a simple spreadsheet or a downloaded budget plan (software), break out the costs of your lifestyle on paper. Get a consensus among key decision-makers as to the validity and the sustainability of these numbers, and then set a course to follow the budget going forward. Review it once per year (or as often as necessary for your household to stay on track).

Step #2: Develop a routine. Establish the accounts necessary to promote your objectives. There is no such thing as the perfect set of accounts or funding plans, only the need for you to have your accounts deal with the short-term, mid-term, and long-term realities of your life goals. A trusted financial professional can help with this task, relative to funding levels (given your budget), investment outcomes, and tax management. At this point, it is most important to have the infrastructure in place and "just do" the work of putting money away each month. This infrastructure and routine promotes great habits for Phase II of your financial life, where the production of income and the accumulation of assets becomes the primary focus.

Step #3: Insure the future. Carry a maximum amount of life insurance and long-term disability insurance. A maximum amount of life and disability insurance does not mean the most offered by your employer, although those amounts (and the price) are important to know. It means carry as much as you can reasonably justify and is allowed by law. Most people have to purchase a life and/or disability insurance supplement to reach these limits.

The Life Cycle of Wealth

If you buy life insurance or a life insurance supplement, be aware that transferring the risk of your death is going to get much more expensive as you age (and get closer to your life expectancy), so buying early means a lower long-term premium. To determine your need for benefits, use one of two general approaches: (1) the replacement cost method or (2) the human life value method. The first method requires calculating the amount of money needed to replace your income for a specified number of years (usually three to seven years), pay off outstanding debts, and educate your children as well as fund any other substantial goals. By contrast, the second method establishes and insures the total value of your lifetime income, arriving at what is typically a higher coverage level. Which approach you use is between you and your insurance professional. Just know that if you die prematurely, there will not be any explanation needed as to why you carried the maximum death benefit under either approach.

Long-term disability insurance or a disability insurance supplement should also be purchased as early in life as possible, although for a different reason. This is a health insurance product that insures your income against morbidity risk (the risk you would contract a condition rendering you unable to work). If you do not purchase the amount of long-term disability insurance needed to reach the legal limit (approximately two-thirds of your pre-tax or gross income) and then have any major health problems, you may be unable to attain the needed coverage. Also, maximizing a long-term disability plan does not just include present benefit levels (based upon your current income), but future levels as well. It is possible for your current policy to offer increase options that would accommodate future growth in your income without requiring you to get a new policy.

Finally, working with an experienced, independent insurance professional on these matters is of the utmost importance. These are the professionals that can access more than one insurance company and force a competitive scenario that benefits you, not the insurance company. In terms of experience, the ideal independent life/disability insurance professional would have five or more years of experience and carry a related professional designation (see Chapter 8, "Finding Your Fiduciary"). However, as long as your professional can assist you in finding the most cost-effective options for a given level of benefits, you are normally getting excellent help. No matter who you work with on this part of your planning, be sure to ask your professional to analyze your employer-based options and your current budget before you apply for private coverage.

Step #4: Install an initial estate plan. The pieces of a basic estate plan include: a final will, powers of attorney, and a living will. A final will serves to instruct the probate court after you have passed away, identifying your personal representative (executor/executrix), naming of custodians (caretakers), beneficiaries (inheritors), and generally directing the distribution of your estate. Powers of attorney give specific authority to other individuals to handle your affairs while you are alive, but unavailable or incapable of representing yourself. Finally, a living will (also called a "medical directive") directs your physicians regarding your end-of-life decisions. If the end of your life is imminent, a living will instructs physicians as to whether or not life support and/or artificial nourishment should be used.

Like other forms of modular planning, it is possible to get basic estate planning documents from the Internet. However, an estate attorney will offer experience and customization not usually available from a web-based template framed from a question and answer session. As an alternative to attempting a self-directed

The Life Cycle of Wealth

estate plan, find an estate attorney that offers a free consultation, then determine your options and the necessity of an attorney/client relationship *prior* to drafting anything yourself. Another cost-cutting measure would be to explore the question-and-answer portion of the self-directed estate planning Web sites, and perhaps even pay for drafted documents. You will then have spent the time developing your intentions and getting an understanding of the process before you meet with an attorney—particularly if they charge by the hour.

Regardless of how you arrive at the final documents needed for a basic estate plan, be sure that those documents get completely executed. Most states require a notary public and/or witnesses to your signature(s) to validate the endorsement of your documents. Once executed, store your estate plans in a safe deposit box or a fireproof safe, along with your life/disability insurance policies, and other vital records (i.e., birth/marriage certificates, social security cards, etc.). Also, inform the key people in your plans about the location of your records and about their role in your plans—during and after your life. Like any other part of your plans, your insurance and estate plan should both be reviewed regularly to accommodate updates and changes to your life, especially if there are major life events, such as a divorce or the death of a family member (or other key person in your plans).

In summary, these four steps do not represent a complete list of everything that could be done to build the infrastructure of your financial life. However, if you get organized, develop a financial routine, insure the future, and enact a basic estate plan, you will have laid the necessary groundwork to move comfortably into Phase II. You will be able to focus on the important task of using your income to build your assets and build-out a written strategic plan.

Phase II: Produce

Transitioning to Phase II is typically a seamless, even unnoticeable process. Like other transitions, there is no exact age at which Phase II occurs, and like other phases, it is unique in its characteristics. These characteristics often include: a higher income, a new home, and perhaps children. While such life changes are positive and exciting, they also represent complexity (even chaos)—a new development that can last for decades.

Recall that Phase I was more focused on the infrastructure of your financial life: getting organized, developing a routine, insuring the future, and having basic estate plan documents drafted. To build upon Phase I, the process of developing a written strategic plan needs to be undertaken during Phase II and address three areas: (1) producing income, (2) managing tax liability, and (3) accumulating assets. While these are very straightforward considerations, they are typically poorly coordinated. Families may end up coordinating their own advisory team—insurance, financial, tax, etc.—which leads to inconsistent planning and more room for headaches in the future. To add consistency, try to identify and work with a primary advisor on your overall plans.

With your primary advisor, Phase II strategic planning will inevitably mean tax planning and investment planning, both of which can simplify the new complexities of this phase. Note that an investment plan by itself does not mean you have an overall financial strategy (it means you are likely focused on holdings first). The investment plan simply funds your overall strategy on a lifelong basis.

However, there is one point regarding your investment plan that should save you a great deal of time, energy, and frustration: to maintain your investment plan over long periods of time, it is essential to understand that market cycles are repetitive and acknowledge that this part market cycle is *not* different, even if it *feels* different. The economic circumstances, headlines, and even the extremity of market movements may be different, but the market cycle itself is not. So the greatest investment idea, market trend, or economic news flash should have little bearing on your long-term results in the financial markets—markets which have repeated the same general historical pattern since returns have been recorded and analyzed dating back over eighty years (Morningstar/Ibbotson, *Stocks, Bonds, Bills & Inflation 1929–2012*). If your investment plan truly is not working, here are some questions you can answer at any phase of the Life Cycle to determine the cause of any portfolio deficiencies:

1. Have I viewed all of my assets in one place on an ongoing basis?
2. What is my overall asset allocation plan?

3. What are the relevant areas of the market with which to compare my portfolio?
4. What is the role of my financial professional(s)?
5. Does my financial professional(s) see a deficiency? If so, what are the recommended changes to be made?
6. If I have an actively managed portfolio, who are the ultimate asset managers (i.e., daily decision makers)? How have they managed risk/reward versus relevant market categories?

Answering these questions will ensure you reach a solid understanding of the issues affecting your portfolio and whether or not adjustments are truly in order. In some cases, no changes are required at all. In many cases, you may need to make adjustments to the portfolio itself or perhaps even change your financial professional relationship(s).

A discussion of Phase II would not be complete without addressing two unique challenges that normally occur during this phase: managing expenses and maintaining habits.

Challenge #1: Manage expenses and invest the cost savings.

I have met many multimillionaires who never made a six-figure income. Instead, they focused on managing their expenses first. You do not hear enough about these people. They typically have the following habits in place:

1. They have a written budget that household decision-makers are all informed of and generally follow. Of course, exceptions are made where necessary.
2. They make a point to live on one income (if there are two incomes present).

3. They buy used cars. The operative words here are *buy* and *used*. Financed or not, many millionaires make a point to own their vehicles and acquire them used, so as to let someone else accept the depreciation involved. With rare exception, they do not rent (i.e., lease) these depreciating assets that are relatively expensive to maintain in the first place.
4. They use savings from the previous three activities to build their assets by investing their money. Successful asset-builders leverage a company retirement plan (especially where a match and/or profit sharing is present), as well as fund IRAs, college savings plans, and nonqualified investment accounts.

Challenge #2: Focus on systematic habits, not holdings.

Unfortunately, you rarely hear the guests at a cocktail party discussing their great investment habits. Instead, you hear about their latest strategy for success, most often centered on a particular holding or idea. Of course, this makes great conversation, but remember, the holdings are infinitely less important than the *habit* of investing on a monthly basis. Too often, radio hosts and financial Web sites glorify their holdings above others (a requirement for them to sell their products or ideas).

So mastering expense management and maintaining great habits are two keys to successfully navigating Phase II. If you can meet these two ongoing challenges, the process of building an overall strategic plan can be more enjoyable. As your budget and habits fuel your plans, you can begin to see your assets accumulate. Tracking your progress along the way, you can even see your own Life Cycle of Wealth unfold. Suddenly, Phase III will become more realistic, more possible, and more exciting.

Phase III: Prosper

The third phase of the Life Cycle is arguably the most exhilarating and full of freedom. Often known as the golden years, this phase is full of renewal. It is a time when many of us see our children become young adults, our careers matured, and our balance sheets enriched. In general, it finds us with a reservoir of energy, with the requisite time and financial means to focus on the things we have waited decades to pursue.

Phase III can also be full of stress, given the life changes and uncertainty involved. From working with many clients crossing from Phase II to Phase III, I know their largest challenge is not the excitement or the affordability of such a transition, but the mental and emotional paradigm shift involved. During Phase I and Phase II, you spend years using income to build your assets. Phase III requires a shift to doing the opposite: using assets to your build income. On the surface, this may not seem like such a big issue, but for those experiencing this transition, it can be overwhelming. Indeed, moving from Phase II to Phase III is often the most challenging financial transition that will occur in a lifetime. The following example illustrates this challenge:

I once accepted a client into my practice who was so invested in his business that he failed to enter Phase III as he planned—twice. He would call and commit to a transition date, then repeatedly back away from it. On his second attempt, he successfully completed the sale of his company and began spending time at his ranch property in Southern Arizona. At his next review meeting, he informed me that he planned to consider a position from a previous competitor and may be headed back to Phase II. I listened, then explained that there was no financial reason for him to make such a move. He agreed, but said, "I'm too full of spit and vinegar to quit now!" For someone who established himself and his business as an industry leader over a thirty-year period, leaving Phase II was especially hard. Thankfully, after his third attempt, he successfully remained in Phase III. Years later, he called me and shared that his wife had just successfully beaten cancer. He was elated that he had remained in Phase III and had a chance to spend quality time with his wife of forty-five years—both before and after her cancer battle.

The point here may be obvious: your Life Cycle will unfold with you or without you. That is not a choice. However, you *can* choose *how* to navigate the Life Cycle. If your pursuit of financial establishment has been secondary to the pursuit of your contribution to the world around you (family, friends, and other loved ones), you will likely have little emotional difficulty transitioning from Phase II to Phase III. However, if you do struggle, understand that you are not alone and you are not crazy. The vast majority of those entering Phase III have to re-examine their priorities as they move forward.

The questions below form a short list of considerations that must be addressed to successfully make the mental and emotional

The Life Cycle of Wealth

leap into Phase III. Answering these questions takes time and energy. It also requires good professional guidance from your financial professional(s).

1. How does my *new* budget look?
2. What are my *new* sources of income?
3. What is the tax treatment of the assets involved?
4. What about health insurance? Long-term care insurance? Life insurance?
5. What are the risk/reward requirements of my investment plan to ensure I have enough assets to live comfortably through Phase IV?
6. If I am successful in Phase III, then how does that affect my estate strategy in Phase IV?

As with other phases, the questions and the answers are often more complex for successful business owners. Much like retiring employees, most business owners who are not retaining control of their enterprise(s) during Phase III will find reassurance about their decisions by answering the six questions above. Some will not. Successful business owners have a financial and an emotional investment in their businesses. While many deserve to retire more than anyone you have met, they often find it hard to let go or reinvest themselves elsewhere. Also, many were not accustomed to investing in a portfolio and grapple with the concept of liquidating their business interests to prepare assets for income distribution.

In some cases, business owners maintain control of their business assets and remain on the company's payroll/benefits plans as long as possible. For those individuals, a Phase III transition really just means working a little less and may not require a great deal of new thinking or planning regarding retirement, with the exception of making pension plan and government entitlement program elections. However, there are many longer-term planning issues for business owners who continue holding their business assets in Phase III and IV, which are outside the scope of this book. It is essential that these individuals seek focused attention regarding their business succession plan and overall estate plan, from competent, experienced advisors.

In summary, Phase III feels like a series of unknowns. Like any other stage of life, there are no guarantees. With the Life Cycle in mind, however, it becomes easier to make the necessary adjustments: to review your plans, reset your expectations, and continue to manage risk. Doing so can make the golden years a reality, and deliver you to Phase IV with confidence.

Phase IV: Preserve

The final phase of the Life Cycle is a very different phase from the first three and is arguably the most complex from a personal and a financial standpoint. Here are a few differences: (1) many life goals have already been accomplished, (2) assets remain readily available for planning, (3) health changes have perhaps become a concern, and (4) adult children are often more involved than before. All of these distinctions make Phase IV unique. Consider the following example of one family's successful Phase IV planning.

Meet Jim, a dear client and friend. He and his wife Jenny ran a multimillion dollar contracting company for decades, and established about $8 million of new wealth for themselves in Phase II. They delayed their entry into Phase III until they were confident they had a well-handled succession plan for their company.

At age seventy, they both fully retired and began the process of using their asset to fund their income. Five years later, Jenny's health began to deteriorate. They agreed to build out a complete estate plan with me and a local estate attorney, then did the hard work of funding that plan.

Jim and Jenny had two children and six grandchildren. They chose a trust-based estate plan and proceeded to draft a revocable living trust with bypass provisions and an irrevocable life insurance trust—both to help mitigate potential estate tax liability. They funded those trusts by organizing assets and retitling them into trust name, according to their financial plans. They also began making annual gifts to their kids and made tuition payments to educational institutions for their grandchildren's post-secondary schooling.

Jenny passed away at age eighty. Since then, Jim has been able to maintain his standard of living and, despite his grief, has continued an abundant retirement in the company of his children and grandchildren. His entire family is completely debt-free, highly educated, and productive members of society, pursuing their own Life Cycles.

When my family relocated across the country in 2009, Jim and other clients were transitioned to another wealth management firm and have maintained their relationship there ever since. As a result, I have not had an opportunity to debrief with Jim about the effectiveness of his and Jenny's estate plans, though I can say with confidence that they did the right initial work of reviewing, structuring, and funding a complete plan that can serve generations of their family, if properly managed by their heirs and their advisors.

Unfortunately, the success that Jim and Jenny enjoyed during their own Life Cycles, as well as the time, energy, and money they spent to ensure their wealth would last for generations, is rare. It is rare because most of us think in terms of what is happening today and relate to it based upon our past experiences. Therefore, thinking in terms of what lies ahead—seriously considering the risks and opportunities present in our own lifetimes and the lifetimes of our children and grandchildren—does not come naturally to most of us.

Jim and Jenny's situation is also rare because not everyone chooses to pay for the advanced planning that characterized their story. Jim currently pays his wealth management firm around $60,000 per year to manage $6MMM of investable assets, out of his total net worth of about $9MM. He has a minimal time commitment for the 99% of the net value he retains (the firm charges approximately 1% per year) and gets an optimal portfolio according to his wishes—something he would have difficulty handling completely on his own. Further, his firm and Jim's outside advisors (estate attorneys, tax accountants) have regular communications with him and his family members about the transition of wealth to future generations, not to mention review meetings with Jim each year. Finally, when the next serious bear market comes, Jim stands a better chance of maintaining his capital with an advisory firm involved, than without one (*Quantitative Analysis of Investor Behavior*, Dalbar, 2013. Print). Indeed, the greatest value proposition the firm can have is its ability to manage downside market risk when the time comes.

While Jim and Jenny were not typical Phase IV clients, their concerns were quite typical. In review meetings, they were consistently interested in the following: (1) how to efficiently transfer wealth from our generation to the next, (2) transferring wealth with minimal administrative and legal requirements for their heirs, and (3) minimizing tax liability in the process. Like any estate planning, their concerns were complex and required input from all other areas of the overall strategic plan: tax, retirement, investments, and insurance.

So detailed estate planning is a process, not an event. It is arguably the most comprehensive *type* of modular planning a family can undertake. Recent financial statements must be updated in to establish net worth and cash flows, and the gross estate must be analyzed. To analyze a gross estate accurately means valuing assets—a process that can take months, particularly where illiquid assets are involved, which require an appraisal (e.g., real estate, personal property, business assets, etc.). After valuations are complete, strategic plan documents can be finalized. After the strategic plan documents are complete, there can be legal plans drafted and funded, which reflect the desires of the individual(s) and can help address the financial/tax consequences involved.

If you have developed wealth in your lifetime and wish to preserve that wealth for your beneficiaries, remember there is a cost. It is true you can spend very little time and money downloading a will from the Internet, filling in the blanks, and executing it at the local bank. However, this does not constitute strategic estate planning. It simply instructs the probate court regarding the appointment of your personal representative (i.e., executor or executrix), the care of any minor children, and the ultimate beneficiaries of your assets. These are important basic steps for any household to take (see Chapter 3, "Phase I: Prepare"). However, strategic estate planning requires a time commitment and it requires some help. It starts with developing a strategy, and it ends with a legacy for your heirs.

Any discussion about building a legacy would not be complete without mentioning trust planning. The decision to build a trust-based plan is different for everyone, although there are four main situations where trust plans are developed: (1) in a blended family arrangement to accommodate prenuptial or other marital agreements regarding asset distribution to separate beneficiaries, (2) to manage state and/or federal estate tax risk, (3) to provide for the care of special needs beneficiaries, and (4) to provide beneficiaries with creditor protection from claims against assets being inherited.

There are generally two types of trusts: revocable and irrevocable. A revocable trust is a grantor trust, meaning the grantors or settlors (the people who established the trust) are the trustees and the assets placed in the trust remain under their control. Further, the income generated from the trust is usually taxable to the grantors/trustees at their own income tax rates. At the death of either the first or second grantor, the trust distributes assets according to the wishes of the settlors to named beneficiaries. An irrevocable trust is a trust where the settlor and the trustee are not the same individual(s). The irrevocable trust is controlled by a party outside the estate, either an individual, a trust company, or both. As an entity separate from and controlled away from the grantors, any assets placed in this type of trust are usually deemed outside the estate of the grantors and income taxable to the trust itself at trust tax rates. These types of trusts are often used to mitigate the effect of projected estate taxes.

Whether an estate plan requires a revocable or an irrevocable trust (or both) is a decision that is usually reached with one's advisors. A CERTIFIED FINANCIAL PLANNER™ professional is trained to properly "map" an estate's projected outcomes, while estate attorneys are trained to draft the legal documents that support these projections. Both professionals tend to be skilled at assisting with trust funding: the process of moving assets into trust title. No matter who assists with trust funding, it is imperative that a trust-based estate plan be funded. An unfunded trust plan means that estate mapping and drafting efforts were completed, but were never used. As such, the reasons to have a trust-based estate plan were not addressed.

Perhaps the most challenging situations I have encountered in estate planning are in working with those holding closely held business interests. For most successfully self-employed families, their enterprise represents both the greatest risk and the best opportunity. This is especially true with estate planning. On one hand, concentrated, illiquid business assets do not tend to transfer as efficiently as liquid assets (especially to more than one beneficiary). On the other hand, the proper transfer of long-term closely held business interests can help mitigate any estate tax issues as well as provide the next generation with wealth from business operations and future growth. The most advantageous steps that established business owners can take in estate planning is to know the value of what they have, develop a written plan to transfer it, and to protect it prior to transfer (in the event of a premature death), and then to fund those objectives.

I started this Chapter by saying, "The final phase of the Life Cycle is a very different phase from the first three..." To consider the movement of wealth forward from Phase IV is the only financial transition that involves an entire family. Due to current tax law, there is also no other transition point in the Life Cycle where a family risks losing such substantial wealth. Many years of hard work, planning, investing, and overall good decision-making can quickly be decimated by taxes, asset sales, and family infighting.

Consider the example of Estee Lauder. When the cosmetic mogul died in 2004, her family was ultimately forced to liquidate 11 million shares of the company in order to meet a $55 million tax liability.
Source: Greg Levine (Forbes, May 18, 2004)

Whether or not you own a closely held business, but especially if you do, a written and funded strategic estate plan is the most important planning process you will ever undertake. The absence of such a plan means putting a substantial piece of a family's hard-earned wealth at risk.

Finally, there is no more emotional form of planning a family can undertake than when it considers the passing of a patriarch/matriarch and the passage of wealth to the next generation. For the passing generation, it is the most selfless planning they will ever complete. Choices made at all other phases of the Life Cycle were necessarily driven by more self-centered "single generation" concerns: their cash flow, their business, their portfolio, their property, their taxes, etc. Other than naming beneficiaries in financial records and in a basic estate plan, there was no concentrated attention given to the needs of their heirs. This makes Phase IV special and requires thinking about the generations of a family.

Managing Risk

At any phase of the Life Cycle, the biggest risk you face is not understanding the risk you already have. In order to understand risk, you have to be able to see it and then be able to manage it. Without proper risk management, even the most advanced, comprehensive financial strategy can fail. So what is risk management and how can it be accomplished?

When you think of risk management, picture a cartoon character trying to plug holes in a leaky dam. As more and more leaks develop, the character is less able to plug each of the holes adequately, jumping from one to the next in an attempt to minimize the damage being caused. Eventually, the overall dam becomes less stable and more susceptible to external (secondary) risks like high winds or tornadoes. The dilemma here is obvious: as more leaks occur, the cartoon character cannot plug all holes and will eventually fail. Eventually, the dam becomes weak and can collapse entirely.

Ideally, the character would have identified any weak spots before the leaks developed, by just stepping back from the dam, looking at the big picture, and solidifying the weak areas. Such a process would logically have prevented the leaks and perhaps avoid a collapse. The same is true of managing risk in your overall strategic plan. It is impossible to identify the weak areas without first viewing all aspects of the big picture: tax, retirement, investments, insurance, and the estate. With at least an informal strategic plan from this exercise, you can begin to clarify your goals and "see" the risk present in them.

Throughout the Life Cycle, there are many different financial risks that need to be identified and managed. Probably the best known example of financial risk is market risk (i.e., non-diversifiable, systematic risk), which comes from supply/demand, prices, inflation, interest rates, and other market-related forces. Another important type of financial risk is unsystematic or "business" risk, which is specific to a particular company or industry and which can be managed through diversification. Such risks include: innovation, competition, management, etc. Other important financial risks include: mortality risk (the risk that you might die), morbidity risk (the risk that you might become disabled), tax risk (the risk that you might unnecessarily pay too much in taxes), longevity risk (the risk you might live too long), and inflation risk (the risk that your purchasing power might erode over time).

The very existence of a written, comprehensive strategic financial plan gives you the ability to see the big picture. This clarity brings about two important dynamics in your plans: (1) it allows you to establish realistic goals based upon complete and detailed data and (2) the primary risks in your plans become obvious. Once you've recalibrated your goals and seen the risk present in them, *doing* risk management becomes more of an art than a science. Your personal values and belief system usually direct the next steps, based upon what is most important to you, so doing risk management becomes a simple checklist of steps to be taken. Examples include: adjusting retirement account contributions, traveling less, establishing a trust, updating insurances, etc.

When you are truly doing risk management with an advisor, you will start to recognize the difference between doing traditional goal-based planning and doing risk-based planning. For example, the traditional goal-based retirement analysis normally includes a question such as: "When would you reasonably like to retire with adequate resources to fund your current standard of living?" Depending upon your response and other preferences, a specific set of recommendations would be generated that would ensure your success of funding the goal of retiring, with little or no attention paid to the major roadblocks to you getting there.

The risk-based approach, however, would not require an initial response from you, but rather seek to understand your financial life such that the answer to the question of when to retire is an output of the overall analysis completed regarding your financial life. In short, the risk-based approach would seek to answer *this* question *for* you: "What are the risks involved with you successfully retiring with the resources necessary to fund your current standard of living?" Although the same parameters, assumptions, and expectations might be used, the final answer to retirement timing could be quite different, but would be the *result* of your working under a risk-focused process.

Moving from a goal-based to a risk-based approach means doing more than running calculations from a series of data inputs.

It requires the interactive exchange of information designed to provide the optimal answers to the big questions, such as "when should I retire?" It means allowing the process to answer questions for you rather than you answering questions for it. It also means you get to *see* risk along the way and make decisions about how to navigate it.

Finding the right advisor is the key ingredient to a successful comprehensive risk management recipe over the long-term. Unfortunately, this search is often confusing and time-consuming. For starters, consider finding a professional that practices risk management rather than someone who *sells* risk management in the form of products, services, and related forms of modular (i.e., partial) planning. Although many professionals practice risk management, it can be difficult to find those who are comprehensive in their work.

A firm that offers comprehensive risk management is usually an advisory firm, a wealth management firm, or a family office. Financial professionals that may practice comprehensive risk management include CERTIFIED FINANCIAL PLANNER™ professionals, CPA/PFS professionals, or other comprehensive advisory professionals. For a complete review of the various types of professionals and firms available to you, see Chapter 8, "Finding Your Fiduciary."

For those financial professionals who understand it, selling risk management products (i.e., insurance products) and practicing risk management (i.e., strategic design and implementation) are separate professions. The person *selling* risk management is interested in your outcomes, but has an inherent conflict with his/her role as a salesperson. The person who *practices* risk management is formalizing a strategy and usually works under a fiduciary standard of practice. Almost everything about these two groups is different: the regulations that govern them, their methods of compensation, and the experience you have. So understand whether you are working with a salesperson selling risk management products or with a true advisor constructing and implementing a risk management strategy.

Regardless of the type of professional(s) you engage, there are multiple types of risks that are ultimately your own responsibility to be aware of and address. For the sake of simplicity, we will consider financial risks as either (1) primary or (2) secondary. Primary risks are the major and relatively predictable risks that you face at each stage of your Life Cycle. These are the risks that, when recognized, can be managed. By contrast, secondary risks are external events beyond your control. These risks are more difficult to manage because they are relatively unpredictable—they are not associated with any particular stage of your Life Cycle and have a lower probability of occurrence than primary risks. Examples of secondary risks would be: car accidents, lawsuits, natural disasters, war, acts of God, etc. Some secondary risks are insurable (e.g., car accidents or natural disasters) while others are not (e.g., war or acts of God). Whether or not we have adequate insurance for the secondary risks, we all need liquidity and flexibility in our plans. This is a major reason why so many financial professionals talk about the importance of an emergency fund to handle the unpredictable risks that occur randomly and present significant short-term expenses.

I spent about two years consulting for a multi-line insurance company and would often get the question from its clients: "What type of short-term disability insurance can I buy?" While there are as many short-term disability insurance policy options as there are agents ready to sell them, the best answer to funding short-term disability needs is have an emergency fund. A short-term disability is an unpredictable risk that, when it occurs, means you cannot work for up to 120 days. It is not specific to any particular phase of the Life Cycle (except to say that it is unlikely you would be employed during Phase IV) and is therefore best managed in a financial plan by simply having a savings account.

Although both primary and secondary risks can derail your plans, primary risks can be dealt with more directly through a strategic planning process because they are more predictable than secondary risks. The following chart summarizes the primary risks associated with each phase of the Life Cycle. This summary is not intended to be an exhaustive list of the possible primary risks you might face at a particular phase, but depicts the most common primary risks associated with each phase. You will see that some primary risks are *phase risks* (e.g. cash flow in Phase I) meaning they are associated primarily with a particular phase, while others are *full-cycle risks*, which are associated with multiple phases (e.g., inflation risk in all phases). Keep in mind that a risk being associated with one phase or another does not make it exclusive to that phase (e.g., funding in Phase II), but rather represents the point at which, should the worst happen, it would have a devastating effect on your overall plans.

The Life Cycle of Wealth

Primary Risk Summary

Phase I: Prepare

Business*
Morbidity
Mortality
Unemployment
Market
Inflation
Cash Flow
Medical Costs

Phase II: Produce

Business*
Income Tax
Gift/Estate Tax
Accumulation
Morbidity
Mortality
Unemployment
Market
Inflation
Cash Flow
Medical Costs

Phase III: Prosper

Business*
Income Tax
Gift/Estate Tax
Estate Transfer
Distribution
Longevity
Long-term Care
Market
Inflation
Cash Flow
Medical Costs

Phase IV: Preserve

Business*
Income Tax
Gift/Estate Tax
Estate Transfer
Distribution
Longevity
Long-term Care
Market
Inflation
Cash Flow
Medical Costs

*This is a unique risk carried by investors with little or no diversification and/or by owners of closely-held businesses.

Some planning professionals will be quick to point out that the correlation between the four phases and the primary risks identified will vary widely from one individual (or family) to the next. They would be right. Financial planning as a process does not change, but the people involved and the data inserted into that process vary widely from one household to the next. As a result, there cannot be a finite list of phase risks. The list above represents a general list of common themes that frequently arise during a strategic planning process.

While there is no perfect method of planning for primary risks at any phase, there are clear steps that can provide for adequate risk management: (1) have a written plan or strategy, (2) based upon your current phase, determine which primary risks on which you need to focus, and (3) make informed decisions with qualified advisors. Regardless of whether a phase risk or a full-cycle risk is involved, taking these three steps will provide the highest possible assurance of safety in your overall strategic plan.

To further distinguish between phase risk and full-cycle risks, consider the following example regarding market risk: a well-known full-cycle risk.

In 2006, I worked with a client named Jamie. I drafted her financial strategy and then worked with her to fund the strategy—aligning her assets and cash flows with her financial plan documents. She called the next year between review meetings and informed me she had attended a seminar for equity indexed annuities and that she needed to reposition half of her $600,000 nest egg into an equity indexed annuity (at the suggestion of the seminar host, an insurance professional). She said "it just [felt] like the safe thing to do."

Jamie was trying to manage market risk late in Phase II (pre-retirement) by transferring the market risk to the proposed insurance carrier, using a deferred annuity contract. The tradeoff? Although her principal would not move downward during a declining market, she was limited to 5% growth over a ten-year time period, during which she would have limited access to her capital. She was sixty years old at the time, retiring in less than five years. With returns limited to a maximum of 5%, her average expected contract return was approximately 2 to 3% over the ten-year period—perhaps enough to cover the effects of inflation on her principal. Not only did her strategic plan require a minimum annual return of 6% on her assets over time, but this limited return potential meant any withdraws she took would be taken from principal. Both points made the annuity contract contrary to decisions she made in the strategic planning process.

Like many of us making a financial decision, Jamie became fixated on managing just one type of risk rather than managing overall risk in her strategic plan. Why? Financial decisions are emotional decisions. Emotions are not rational, and so risk management can quickly become impossible, without the right advisor(s) *and* the right strategic plan(s).

Furthermore, if managing market risk was, in fact, the only consideration (i.e., Jamie was completely uncomfortable taking market risk in Phases III and IV), the annuity would be one option to protect the principal value of her assets. For principal protection, Jamie might also consider some alternatives: bank CDs, bonds, unit investment trusts, or principal-protected notes, to name a few. The salesperson hosting the event did not mention these options because he was not compensated to do so, but therein lies the difference between selling risk management and practicing risk management.

The takeaway: Whether or not she made decisions in line with her strategic plan, Jamie was dealing with a full-cycle risk.

She could approach market risk many different ways and with many different vehicles, all of which have pros and cons. The key for Jamie to navigate these options: knowing her current phase, which primary risks are involved, and then deciding—in light of her overall strategy—upon the best possible course of action to manage those risks.

Phase risks and full-cycle risks must be treated with the same amount of careful consideration. Remember that *any* primary risk—phase risk or full-cycle risk—is primary because it represents the possibility of an entire strategic plan being ruined. Consider the following example of long-term care risk—a primary risk in Phases III and IV.

Matthew and his wife Cathy made great strides in their financial establishment late in Phase II. Now in their mid-sixties and having successfully crossed into Phase III, they consciously decided to self-insure the financial risk of needing long-term care later in life. They understood that the average risk for their situation would have a 70% chance of occurring if they both reached age sixty-five and that the average cost of such events would range from $150 to $250,000 each, based on the lifestyle they intend to maintain.* In order to completely self-insure such a need, they established a separate account and funded it with $400,000. The funds are invested to grow for their heirs unless needed during their lifetimes to fund care expenses. Needless to say, Matthew and Cathy have identified a risk and have dealt with it in a realistic fashion. In fact, the additional $400,000 they needed to manage long-term care risk was built into their retirement requirements to ensure they did not retire with assets less than was needed to handle both their retirement cash flow projections, in addition to their long-term care risk.

*2013, US Department of Health and Human Services (www.longtermcare.gov)

The Life Cycle of Wealth

By contrast, I have talked with many individuals who wish to self-insure their long-term care risk without separate funding like Matt and Cathy. Even knowing the amount of expense and likelihood of occurrence, they chose to self-insure using the same assets intended to fund their retirement income needs. Clearly, this scenario means accepting too much primary risk. Should any need for care arise—assisted living, nursing home, custodial, or hospice care—the strategic plan is compromised because assets intended to provide retirement income are spent down, and longevity risk (the risk of outliving one's assets) becomes a major issue.

Self-insurance is one option when addressing any insurable primary risk. As an alternative, Matt and Cathy could have chosen to partially or completely transfer risk through the purchase of insurance against the financial risk of long-term care events. In this case, they would choose to pay premiums into a policy that would pay benefits in the event of their need for care. Like other insurance, the decision to purchase, along with the qualifications of acceptance, are as specific as the people involved and therefore beyond the scope of this text. However, it is important to distinguish between self-insuring (i.e., paying cash) and transferring risk through insurance (i.e., paying a premium). Finally, it is essential to compare the pros and cons involved, and make a conscious decision about whether to self-insure or not. Whatever the final decision, the risk must be managed, and it must be managed in the context of a larger strategic plan.

So how does one get to "see" risk? Primary risks can be evaluated and managed through the overall strategic planning process (see Chapter 2, "Making Great Strategy Decisions"). First, have an understanding of your current position on the Life Cycle. Second, have a written strategy to answer important planning questions, such as when to retire, what house to buy, how much life insurance you need, etc. Third, get at least a basic understanding both types of primary risks you face—phase risks and full-cycle risks. Following this process will illuminate the primary risks you face. Note that secondary risks are more difficult to see, as they are less predictable and therefore difficult to plan for (although some are insurable). Finally, the secret to seeing and then managing primary risks is to engage the right professionals to assist you along the way.

Finding Your Fiduciary

I once had a successful real estate developer ask me why he should pay a financial services firm for its expertise. I told him that "from a planning standpoint, you will likely pay less in taxes, insurance premiums, and probate costs. From an investment management standpoint, you will likely take less risk, get a better return, or both. The tough part is seeing past the short-term to understand the long-term value of what's being offered." Seeing long-term value has everything to do with understanding which professional(s) to engage. Therefore, deciding which financial professional(s) to engage is perhaps the most important decision you will make during your Life Cycle.

The importance of this decision is probably the most evident with investment outcomes. DALBAR, Inc. conducts an annual investor behavior study, entitled *Quantitative Analysis of Investor Behavior* (2013, www.dalbar.com). This advanced research has consistently demonstrated that over the past twenty years, individual investors who did *not* work with a financial professional have underperformed major market indexes between 3.96% and 5.36% versus their peers who *did* work with a professional.

Unfortunately, the decision about which professional(s) to engage (and for which purpose) can also be the most confusing. There are only subtle differences in the titles and descriptions used by financial professionals to describe themselves and their offerings, yet there are major differences in the types of professionals and the types of products and services they provide. What follows is a brief explanation of the five different types of financial professionals you may choose to engage. While this is by no means an exhaustive list of financial professionals and their differences, it is adequate for understanding the general categories of professionals that are available for you to engage, and what to expect when you do.

The Insurance Professional

Who they are: This type of financial professional is obviously an excellent resource for protecting that which is most important to you—your family, your income, your homes, cars, etc. I have met countless caring, hardworking, and well-informed insurance professionals in the past fifteen years. They are among the most well-meaning type of financial professional you can engage and a good resource for making insurance product decisions: property/casualty, life, health, etc.

What they do: This professional is often the most product-driven financial professional you could engage. To the extent you need to buy a product (policy, annuity, etc.), this group is typically going to move heaven and earth to get it for you and probably do so competitively.

Recognize, though, that their knowledge may be limited to the products they sell. Getting objective advice or financial planning accomplished with your insurance professional can be quite difficult, if not impossible.

How they think: It has been said that to be successful in the insurance industry, the professional must "have the heart of a social worker and the mind of a capitalist." This is perhaps the most accurate description of the best insurance professionals I have met. They have a great deal of care and concern for their customers and a great deal of motivation to drive their own income.

How they sound: The insurance community is trained to offer programs and solutions that provide protection or a guarantee. It tends to refer to customers rather than clients, although both terms might be used. They tend to talk about products that they are excited about for one reason or another. Finally, insurance professionals use a great deal of material to market their products. This material may include references to "financial services" and "your financial future." The insurance professional may carry any number of professional designations, which may include, but are certainly not limited to, any of the following: CLU, ChFC, AAI, ACSR, AIP, a.m. CEBS, CIC, CISR, CPCU, CPSR, LUTCF, REBC, RHU, AAI.

How they are paid: Insurance professionals are compensated primarily by commissions paid on the insurance plans they sell. As a result, they maintain relationships entirely with those customers and/or referral sources who provide them with a continuous source of new business. If they are relatively new to the financial services industry, they may be quite aggressive in order to maintain a steady cash flow in the short-term.

The Brokerage Professional

Who they are: This is the type of financial professional that is in the business of transacting securities products: stocks, bonds, mutual funds, variable annuities, etc. They, like the insurance professionals, are not likely to give advice or practice financial planning. The brokerage professional is typically newer to the investment side of the financial services industry than their advisory and wealth management peers, although often very capable. This is a great professional to engage for a specific investment product need.

What they do: The brokerage professional often has great ideas and solutions (i.e., products) for a specific need. They are used to opening and funding accounts and handling orders. They aren't necessarily active traders, but may carry a transactional mind-set. For those that offer client reviews, they typically do so with the idea of measuring the success of previous transactions and with the hope of developing more transactional business.

How they think: Regardless of age or experience, brokers are the purist of capitalists and therefore quite opportunistic—for their clients and for themselves. In many cases, they have made a great deal of their own money and become encouraged by their own success, believing they can bestow that success upon their clients.

How it sounds: The brokerage community talks about investment products. A broker is most likely to call you with a tip, an opportunity, or an idea. If they are experienced at their work, they almost always discuss their years of experience. And while the brokerage professional may carry any number of professional designations, he/she is much more likely to talk about their specific expertise versus their academic pursuits. Finally, they are referred to as representatives, registered representatives, or financial representatives. This is appropriate, given they are representing a particular firm and its products. Also, most broker/dealers (i.e., brokerage) firms and their representatives are members of the Financial Industry Regulatory Authority (FINRA) and the Securities Investor Protection Corporation (SIPC). So when you see FINRA or SIPC, you are probably dealing with a brokerage professional.

The various types of brokerage licenses and compensation arrangements that brokers and their firms work under are beyond the scope of this text. However, it is important to know that there is a progression of knowledge among brokerage professionals based on which licenses they hold. Most brokers carry a FINRA Series 7 (General Securities Representative) license, although some carry a FINRA Series 6. Additional state-level licensing requirements include either a FINRA Series 63 or 66. The following link provides a breakdown of common securities licenses held by practicing brokerage professionals: http://www.investopedia.com/articles/financialcareers/07/securities_licenses.asp#axzz276h4JNMm

It is also important to note that brokerage professionals are obligated to meet the requirements of their firm and the Securities Exchange Act of 1934 (the 1934 Act) as well as the regulatory organizations that enforce the 1934 Act. The overall regulator of the securities industry is the Securities and Exchange Commission (SEC), which was created by the 1934 Act; however, the Financial Institution Regulatory Authority (FINRA) is the primary enforcer of brokerage regulations for the SEC. FINRA is an independent privately held corporation contracted by the SEC to carry out enforcement duties under the 1934 Act. Therefore, FINRA is employed by the SEC. For more information about FINRA, please visit www.finra.org. For more information about the SEC, visit www.sec.gov.

It is also important to know whether the professional works with an independent brokerage firm, a traditional brokerage firm, or a bank or insurance company (see "Appendix II - Questions to Ask a Financial Professional). If the distinctions are not already clear to you, an independent firm will typically have the most objective view in servicing its clients. A traditional brokerage firm is engaged with both the primary and secondary markets, meaning they are in the business of underwriting and distributing initial securities offerings (primary markets) as well as acting as broker/dealer after the securities are offered (secondary markets). The traditional brokerage firm is highly profit driven and therefore more focused on serving clients for the sake of making money than for improving client outcomes. An institution-owned brokerage firm tends to view their brokerage business as a revenue enhancement (banks) or a necessary evil (insurance companies) or both. Most do not focus on their brokerage business on a primary basis and, therefore, offer a more limited menu of options to customers. Also, their culture is similar to a traditional brokerage firm in that they are more driven by the financials of having the brokerage for customers, than they are in improving the outcomes of their customers.

How they are paid: Traditional brokerage professionals are paid a commission for transacting securities business. Changes in technology have provided a more fluid option for brokers and their clients, known as a "wrap fee" or a fee in lieu of a commission. This wrap fee is not the same as an advisory fee, although the two feel quite similar to investors. Note that brokers may be paid a commission on some products or accounts, and a wrap fee on others.

The Advisory Professional

The advisory professional and the brokerage professional are often confused with one another, for two reasons: (1) many financial professionals are both brokerage and advisory professionals and (2) whether or not the financial professional is practicing as both, the various titles carried by these individuals are similar, if not identical. The following is a brief summary of the distinctions of an advisory professional.

Who they are: The advisory professional is typically a seasoned financial professional, usually a broker and/or insurance professional who may still maintain those licenses and activities, but who typically works on a fee basis, rather than a commission basis. Their fee may be charged as a fee on assets in an investment advisory engagement or an hourly fee for consulting, research, projects, etc. Note that "fee-based" normally references an advisory professional that works under a combination of fees and commissions, with a priority on their fee business. A "fee-only" advisor, by comparison, works without *any* commissions from insurance or investment activities.

What they do: The primary distinction of an advisory professional is they are in the business of giving advice. Remember that advice does not generate a commission, only products carry commissions. Purchasing products and receiving advice may go hand-in-hand;

however, they are not the same thing. It is important to note that a "fee-based" (advisory and brokerage both) or "fee-only" (advisory only) professional is putting their advisory work ahead of their brokerage business and for good reason. Products are only products until they follow advice. If products follow advice, they become solutions.

Advisory professionals must adhere to the Investment Advisors Act of 1940, which, among other requirements, mandates that Investment Advisors and their Representatives conduct business under a fiduciary standard of practice. In other words, these professionals must act "as if a trustee" for their clients. From the Latin word *fides*, *fiduciary* literally means "faith" and "trust." By comparison, the 1934 Act requires brokerage professionals to maintain suitability ("good fit") standard, but not necessarily a fiduciary standard.

With the 2010 passage of the Dodd-Frank Act, Congress took steps toward unifying financial professionals around a common fiduciary standard, giving the SEC authority to impose such a universal requirement on all retail investment professionals. As of this writing, such a uniform standard has *not* been enacted, due in large part to ongoing debate about the enforcement, compliance, and business implications for brokerage firms and their brokers.

How they think: The advisory professional often views their role as that of a partner to their clients. The phrase "personal CFO" is used frequently, likely because of the strong relationships that advisory professionals build with their clientele. They don't typically view themselves as salespeople, and although most want to grow their business, that is not necessarily their drive. They are driven instead by new client relationships that are mutually fruitful over time.

How it sounds: Advisory professionals have a genuine desire to better the lives of others, hence their decision to work under a fiduciary standard. As a result, you may hear about them talk about "helping others" or "doing work for others." This is a genuine belief (as opposed to a sales pitch, which some financial salespeople also use). The easiest way to identify the advisory professional is to meet with multiple financial services offices. Those that do not immediately invite you to do new business or discuss products are likely the true advisory offices. Rather than concerning themselves with generating revenue, they instead ask questions in an attempt to learn about you and probably schedule a follow-up appointment to discuss ideas and opportunities.

How they are paid: Advisory professionals are paid a fee on assets or a fee for planning, perhaps both. As a result, they do not think in terms of products, transactions, and commissions, but in terms of the asset base or plan that they are following. This is an important distinction for those seeking an advisor versus a brokerage professional often referred to as an advisor.

THE WEALTH MANAGEMENT PROFESSIONAL

The wealth management professional or "wealth manager" was born out of the advisory profession and shares many characteristics with the advisory professional. The primary two distinctions of a wealth manager are education and experience. These professionals typically carry advanced financial designations and have a long-term background in financial services.

Consequently, the wealth management profession is occupied by the most capable professionals, although they are unlikely to take credit for this fact.

Who they are: The hallmark of wealth management is strategy design and implementation. Wealth managers operate primarily (or entirely) under the Advisors Act of 1940 and share the same relationship-based approach as advisory professionals. However, their ability to deliver strategy is what sets them apart from the other types of financial practitioners. Strategy capabilities may not be easy to identify, especially given that advisory professional and wealth management professional share most of the same traits, and advisory professionals will often use the same marketing nomenclature or even call themselves wealth managers.

What they do: True wealth managers actually do what they advertise: manage wealth. In doing so, they provide a big picture financial view to higher-net-worth clients than do other financial professionals. This holistic view is based in comprehensive planning but provides the estate, tax, retirement, insurance, and investment strategy needed to navigate that big picture. Other financial professionals do not tend to provide holistic strategy.

How they think: Wealth managers tend to view themselves as a resource for their clients. They do not view themselves as product distributors or salespeople. Many do not even carry brokerage licenses and therefore charge only an hourly and/or asset-based fee as opposed to accepting a commission for their work. They think in terms of building lasting relationships with their clients through regular communication and meetings.

How it sounds: It may be impossible to tell the difference between the advisory professional and the wealth management professional on the surface. One sure way to know is to inquire as to whether or not the professional offers holistic planning in addition to investment management. If tax, estate, retirement, and insurance are all discussed—in addition to investments—then you are likely working with a true wealth management professional. Also look for advanced financial designations such as CFP® (CERTIFIED FINANCIAL PLANNER™), CFA (Chartered Financial Analyst), and CPA/PFS (Certified Public Accountant/Personal Financial Specialist), which require professionals to successfully complete comprehensive exams in order to become designated. Although there are many impressive professionals and other available designations, these are examples of designations often found with advanced financial professionals. Remember that years of experience and advanced designations are also strong indication of whether or not wealth management describes the actual client experience or is simply a marketing approach.

How they are paid: Wealth managers are paid in a variety of ways, most often on a fee-basis similar to advisory professionals. However, actual wealth management is a multidisciplinary profession so may include more services with varying methods of compensation, which depend upon the client engagement. For example, some wealth management firms are fee-only regarding their handling of assets and their planning activities, but offer insurance as a means of completing business and estate plans. This translates to a "fee-based" (versus "fee-only") method of compensation.

Aaron D. Kolkman

The Family Office Professional

This type of professional is the one you are least likely to meet or hear about. This is because they work for a very small number of clients or perhaps just one. For example, Bill and Melinda Gates have a family office that handles their financial concerns—including trust administration, paying bills, filing taxes, conducting planning, handling assets, and any other work relative to the family's financial well-being.

As you might expect, there are few of these professionals (because there are few clients in this category). Their practices vary widely and are generally less regulated than other areas of the financial industry. As a result, some hedge funds have considered refiling with the SEC as family offices to lessen their regulatory requirements.

This area of the financial services business is evolving quickly and is one that many long-term professionals aspire to. However, it remains much less commonplace and is therefore largely beyond the scope of this text.

CREATING RECURRENCE

Every financial office I have worked in and every one I have visited has talked regularly about multigenerational wealth transfers. However, if you interview ten financial offices, few will offer complete strategic planning in this area. Even when this sort of advanced planning is present, there are no guarantees that the design, implementation, and outcomes will work precisely as intended. In fact, a written estate strategy (i.e., design) with proper legal structure and adequate funding (i.e., execution) can fail to operate as intended.

In 2003, Roy Williams and Vic Preisser interviewed 3,250 families and discovered that 30% of estate plans generally succeeded while 70% of wealth transitions failed (*Preparing Heirs*, Robert D. Reed, 2003, Print). Rather unexpectedly, Williams and Preisser's work demonstrated that such failures were *not* caused primarily by planning mistakes, poor advice, complexity, health problems, or even economics. In fact, tax, legal, and legacy planning issues contributed to only 15% of the failures involved. The other 85% of wealth transition failures were caused by two *qualitative* factors:

- 60% of all wealth transition failures were caused by a breakdown of communication and/or trust within the family unit in general, across generations.
- 25% of all such failures were caused by inadequately prepared heirs, which also stemmed from a breakdown of communication and/or trust, this time among beneficiaries.

So among the 85% of those families whose estate plans failed, a proper plan design and execution had been completed. Despite having a written strategic plan, legal drafting, and proper funding, the failure still occurred due a breakdown in *family dynamics.*

There is no simple answer to managing the family dynamics involved in an estate planning process. However, there are two simple points which will assist in managing this challenge: (1) family dynamics must be considered a real and primary risk in Phases 3 and 4 (a.k.a. "Estate Transfer" Risk, see Chapter 7, Primary Risk Summary Chart) and (2) professional advisors must understand such a qualitative risk cannot be managed through a technical planning process. In general, advisors must facilitate a shift from quantitative planning to qualitative planning, although both the family and its advisors must make a concerted effort to identify those dynamics that might ambush an otherwise technically sound plan for multigenerational wealth.

To summarize, Williams and Preisser found that 15% of wealth transfer failures are caused by inadequate technical planning (i.e., quantitative factors) while 85% of such failures are attributable family dynamics (i.e., qualitative factors). This means that 85% of the largest financial risk involved in the Life Cycle of Wealth—Estate Transfer Risk—is driven by internal family relationships. If family relationships are the cause of so much financial breakdown, families must recognize and manage this risk if wealth is to successfully move from Phase 4 to the next generation(s).

First, to address the risk of being in the 15% of failures due to inadequate planning: families can develop and maintain a written and funded strategic estate plan. This process is simple, but not easy. It requires a complete inventory of assets and liabilities (i.e., a family balance sheet), an examination of the titling of assets and liabilities, a review of the beneficiaries listed on assets, the implications of probate, and of course, an understanding of the tax consequences of a given strategic plan. Once the estate is detailed in this manner, then the legal structure must be added or changed to accommodate the "flow" of the estate as designated by the strategic design. Finally, the new legal structures must be given life—they must be funded. This can be as simple as rearranging beneficiaries or as complex as placing property in trust title and re-recording deeds. It may also involve the purchase of insurance or other financial products needed to provide the liquidity and/or income needed to make the plan work. These steps—strategy, drafting, and funding—are the cornerstone of a technically sound estate plan. While they may take many months to complete, doing so means that 15% of the Estate Transfer Risk has been managed.

Second, to address the risk of being in the 85% of estate transfer failures, families must simply connect with each other. In general, families need to communicate *across* and *within* generational lines of the family to review details of the plan. Communicating across generations means having open conversations with your children and grandchildren about what has been done, what is intended, and what is expected of both participants and beneficiaries. Communication within generational lines means a couple talking intentionally with each other, or with their siblings, even close friends, also about what has been done, what is intended, and what is expected of everyone involved in the plan.

These communications may seem awkward at first as the subject of estate planning does not often arise in the course of everyday conversations. However, those who spend focused time discussing the big picture plan will insulate themselves from 85% of the greatest financial risk in the Life Cycle. As a matter of practice, consider doing the following: set aside fifteen to twenty minutes during a holiday meal, driving in the car, talking over the phone, or sitting at coffee. Start the initial conversation with something as simple as "I want to make sure you understand what is happening with our family's finances so we can all be on the same page." Then talk about what work has been done to develop, structure, and fund an estate strategy. Also, explain the reasons that the strategy was built the way it was and what is expected of the key participants and beneficiaries. Finally, avoid closing the door to interactive discussion about the strategy and try to welcome feedback. Others may have a new idea to better the plan or perhaps even a different mind-set about what is expected of them.

In some cases, there may be short-term conflict, which can often lead to better overall results for the plan. Such conflicts can bring forward those family dynamics that might otherwise destroy the estate strategy and provide an opportunity to resolve those issues during the lifetimes of those who are building the plan. Whether initial conversations are pleasant or not, welcoming honest feelings and discussion about the family's plans, not only provides for better relationships within the family unit, it helps protect the family

The Life Cycle of Wealth

from Estate Transfer Risk. In the end, a collective peace with the direction of the family's wealth and values is possible.

Using the Life Cycle model in this dialogue can help guide the conversation and contribute to a common view of money and its role in the family tree. Furthermore, the model can facilitate a more rapid understanding about the concepts involved in an estate strategy and reveal the recurring nature of wealth across generations. Perhaps most importantly, the participants in an estate planning process can better comprehend the bigger picture and where they fit in the Life Cycle pattern of their own family.

In 1993, Robert Avery and Michael Rendall of Cornell University estimated that the baby boomers would receive at least $10.4 trillion in inheritances from their parents between 1990 and 2040 (*The Wise Inheritor*, Ann Perry, 2003, Print). Avery and Rendall's analysis was done using the value of a dollar in 1989. Applying a 3% inflation rate, the equivalent value of wealth transfers in 2013 is approximately $18.8 trillion. This enormous intergenerational movement of assets—a process I will refer to as "the great transition"—is the largest of its kind in American history.

If 70% of these wealth transfers are subject to fail during the great transition, then an estimated $13.1 trillion in total value can be deemed at risk. You already know that managing this risk has something to do with written strategic planning, drafting, and funding, and everything to do with maintaining open lines of communication within your family.

Ann Perry wrote from her own experience as a beneficiary, having inherited rights to the classic game "Go Fish" from her grandmother's estate. Throughout her story, Perry makes multiple references to the need for expert advice in the strategic planning process, especially relative to estate planning:

> *It always amazes me that people who would never dream of wiring the electrical outlets in their house or replacing the carburetor on their car will fail to seek financial help. As a society, we believe we should know how to manage money because it's such a part of our everyday lives. Well, so are light sockets and cars, but I'll rely on electricians and mechanics to help me with major repairs. Hiring professionals…to assist you with your investing, taxes and estate planning should greatly help maximize your inheritance.*

If you are the matriarch or patriarch of a family, the most difficult thing about creating recurrence is you will not live to see the wealth transfer process happen. As such, the process of planning multigenerational wealth means seeing a balance sheet as only "yours" for only a short time. To act on such wisdom is to engage in a selfless planning process that benefits others, with no guarantees that your time, energy, and expenses will make your vision a reality. However, managing estate transfer risk substantially increases the likelihood of your wealth doing everything you imagined and more. As my friend Nick Murray reminds us: Wealth is the absence of financial worry, an income you cannot outlive, and an inheritance for your children and grandchildren.

As your Life Cycle of Wealth unfolds, there are many choices to be made—choices about your relationships, your housing, your car, your career, your service providers, your advisors. Every life and every story is unique and so, therefore, are the financial considerations. Understanding wealth as *financial establishment*, viewing it as a means to an end, and treating it as a universal language will equip you with clarity to make great financial decisions. Putting your purpose on paper by developing a written strategic

The Life Cycle of Wealth

plan with your trusted advisor(s) means you enhance your clarity and add technical knowledge from which to make those decisions. Finally, remembering the Life Cycle image as a long-term process of managing risk to achieve your dreams brings the perspective you need to successfully complete the journey and increase the likelihood of delivering your wealth forward for generations.

Appendix I – Quantitative Analysis of Investor Behavior (Dalbar, 2013.)

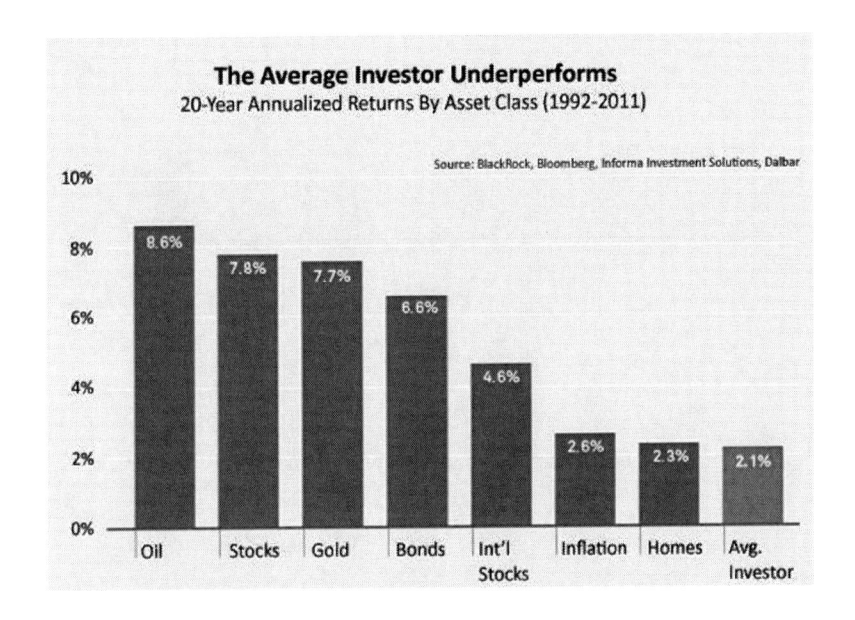

The Average Investor Underperforms
20-Year Annualized Returns By Asset Class (1992-2011)

Source: BlackRock, Bloomberg, Informa Investment Solutions, Dalbar

Asset Class	Return
Oil	8.6%
Stocks	7.8%
Gold	7.7%
Bonds	6.6%
Int'l Stocks	4.6%
Inflation	2.6%
Homes	2.3%
Avg. Investor	2.1%

Appendix II–Questions to Ask a Financial Professional

1. What is your general background and how many years of experience do you have?
2. What are your specialties, and which designations do you carry?
3. What process or approach do you use in serving clients?
4. How do you manage financial risk for your clients?
5. What product or service offerings do you have?
6. How are you paid?

Appendix III – Financial Designations

Visit: http://www.investopedia.com/articles/01/101001.asp#axzz276h4JNMm

Bibliography

The Alphabet Soup of Financial Certifications. Investopedia, 2013 http://www.investopedia.com/articles/01/101001.asp#axzz 276h4JNMm

Campbell, David. *If you don't know where you are going, you'll probably end up somewhere else.* Valencia: Tabor, 1974. Print.

Carnegie, Dale. *How to Win Friends and Influence People.* 1936. New York: Simon & Schuster, 1981. Print.

Dalbar, Inc. *Quantitative Analysis of Investor Behavior*, 2013. www.dalbar.com.

Hill, Napoleon. *Think and Grow Rich. 1937.* Meriden: The Ralston Society. Print.

Kiyosaki, Robert T. and Lechter. *Sharon L. Rich Dad, Poor Dad.* New York: Warner, 1998. Print.

Levine, Greg. *Lauder: Family Sells Shares For Estee's Estate Tax*, Forbes, May 18, 2004.

Mandino, Og. *The Greatest Salesman in the World*. 1968. New York: Bantam, 1983. Print.

McCormack, Mark. *What They Don't Teach You in the Harvard Business School*. New York: Bantam, 1984. Print.

Morningstar/Ibbotson, *Stocks, Bonds, Bills & Inflation 1929 – 2012*. 2013.

Murray, Nick. *Simple Wealth, Inevitable Wealth*. 1999. New York: Murray, 2010. Print.

Perry, Ann. *The Wise Inheritor*. 2003. New York: Broadway, 2003. Print.

Stanley, Thomas J. and Danko, William D. The Millionaire Next Door. 1996. Marietta: Longstreet. 1998. Print.

US Department of Health and Human Services. Find Your Path Forward, 2013 (www.longtermcare.gov)

Williams, Roy. Preisser, Vic. Preparing Heirs, San Francisco: Robert D. Reed, 2003. Print.